WALKING FOUR WAYS
IN THE WIND

PRINCETON SERIES OF CONTEMPORARY POETS
David Wagoner, *Editorial Adviser*

OTHER BOOKS IN THE SERIES

Returning Your Call, by Leonard Nathan

Sadness And Happiness, by Robert Pinsky

Burn Down the Icons, by Grace Schulman

Reservations, by James Richardson

The Double Witness, by Ben Belitt

Night Talk and Other Poems, by Richard Pevear

Listeners at the Breathing Place, by Gary Miranda

The Power to Change Geography, by Diana Ó Hehir

An Explanation of America, by Robert Pinsky

Signs and Wonders, by Carl Dennis

WALKING FOUR WAYS IN THE WIND

by John Allman

PRINCETON UNIVERSITY PRESS

Publication of this book has been aided by a grant from
the Paul Mellon Fund of Princeton University Press
This book has been composed in V.I.P. Aldus

Clothbound editions of Princeton University Press books
are printed on acid-free paper, and binding materials are
chosen for strength and durability

Printed in the United States of America by Princeton
University Press, Princeton, New Jersey

FOR *Eileen* AND *Jennifer*

Contents

I

II

III

IV

V

Acknowledgments

Poems in this collection appeared originally in the following publications:

The Attic: "On the Roof," "Filling the Straight," "For One Who Moved Away"

The Beloit Poetry Journal: "Release"

The Chowder Review: "Freud's Last Dream," "Geriatrics," "The Fixer," "Gimpel the Fool," "Late Morning," "The Visitors"

Epos: "The Artifice"

Gravida: "Boy," "Finding Them"

Hiram Poetry Review: "A Former Life," "Pumas"

Kansas Quarterly: "Her Repertory"

Northeast: "Departure," "Middle Age"

Paris Review: "The Color of Neville Brand's Front Teeth"

Poetry: "Away & Towards," "Into," "Return"

Poetry Americana: "A Death"

Poetry Northwest: "Creedmoor: The Locked Ward," "Kinship," "The Knuckler," "The Measure of a Dachshund's Jaw," "The Soul Grown Lazy," "Surgery" (under the title "Operation"), "The Weeper," "Wives of Geniuses," "The Ward Wife," "His Cremation," "Personal," "Nana's Visit," "You Owe Them Everything"

Poetry Now: "Losing," "The Soul Plays You Bet Your Life," "The Soul Walks Out"

Rocky Mountain Review of Language and Literature: "The Mild"

Southern Poetry Review: "Widow"

Sunbury: "Widower"

Yes (A Magazine of Poetry): "Cave Paintings"

Some of these poems were written under the auspices of a Faculty Fine Arts Fellowship in poetry granted by the Research Foundation of State University of New York.

I

ON THE ROOF

Natural signals: TV antennas, young trees,
strapped to chimneys; gulls wheeling through
radio waves like blanched crows, as you
lay back in fossil shadows from a lost sea,
impossible imprints in your back. Tar Beach:
the pop of punched metal, spray hissing into wind,
your first beer, and Marge tilted back, joined
to the ledge like a ship's figurehead, within reach,
her wrist North, her elbow South, her knees
to the sun like fists rubbed smooth of knuckles.
Up here, you forgot the deep cry and dry suckle
of baby brothers, you felt your angers unfreeze.
You came to Marge the brown-armed boy from drought-
stricken villages, iceberg lettuce crisp in your mouth.

THE MEASURE OF A DACHSHUND'S JAW

You seemed miles above, Frau Kissel,
yelling down the dumbwaiter shaft,
"What you do down there!" letting
your empty dogfood cans clatter toward us.
You seemed miles below, your voice
rumbling into the furnace
as we stole kisses from the super's Marge,
coal dust on our pants. O the whites
of your eyes, Frau, yellow as rest homes,
awful as grandmothers falling into liquor
stores. You shambled past Mendel's newsstand,
fingers flicking in and out of his money box.

Halloween, you held pennies in tongs
over the stove's hot jets, threw them down
into the alley where we sang like beggars.
Convert to St. Vitas, your touch trembled
like raw eggs in a river. You stretched neighbors'
curtains on your rack of needles, 10¢ an hour.
You clomped on the roof like Mr. Angelo
with stroke, shouting commands at pigeons,
letting loose your dachshund. We saw you
raise a fist to your husband in the sky,
his biplane breaking up over the Argonne,
ripping through calendar pictures of France.

And when you broke your hip on super's
icy sidewalk, no one brought groceries;
did your laundry; walked your dog
the level of a snarl. We left dead mice
at your door: heard you cry out
like the crazy lady in subways.
And months later, after your dachshund
bit Marge, you were yelling at the ASPCA truck

parked near the hydrant; dog biscuits
falling from your bag; money in a white
sweat sock that you swung like a club
beating the air, bruising whatever bruised you.

HER REPERTORY

Uneasy dreams. Gauze over her
mouth: father behind the arras,
hearing confession, giving her
violets on the tip of brother's
poignard. That play again,
like the coughing in tenements,
memories of her mother wheezing.
The boyfriend's back from school,
much taller, roses in his boots,
giving her sonnets & billet-doux:

husband, wanting her demure,
clean as his mother's teeth.
Could she handle his cold
eggs & querulous mornings?
Her father whispers that deceit
is a woman's way, & besides,
that boy has crooked legs,
what would her mother say: bad
genes, bad blood. Marry wealth.
Button up. Keep smiling.

Her fingers close on the paring
knife, lifting it as they enter,
the angel intruders, Welfare men
with flushed cheeks, wings awry.
She's peeling onions, weeping.
Now she's walking in the queen's
garden, in mother's bright shawl.
No fog rolls in, this evening.
Father falls through the privet hedge,
his face blue, choking on a pearl.

CREEDMOOR: THE LOCKED WARD

I ask what she needs
write it down
she can't
her penmanship's
a five-year-old's
hair cut close to her head

mother wants a boy
and who doesn't

weeping into a balled-up tissue
next time bring tissues
and shoes
would I buy brown shoes?

tell mother to call
where is mother
tell mother to forget it

two fat women
in the immense dayroom
waltzing arm in arm
the boy who borrows cigarettes
behind them
singing a hymn

I can't buy shoes
without her feet

she'd give me
her feet

I'm thinking of my wife and daughter
I want to leave

bring tissues

between the casement windows
the young woman laments
    her abortion at 20
    who really had none

    what happened to the dog
    did you put him to sleep
    where is mother?

I look across the room
at the unused pool table
cues lined up dusty as WWI rifles

    small voices weeping
    in my throat

smell cooking smell
canned peas and carrots
Salisbury steak

    thin gravy voice
    of the old schoolteacher
    playing old songs
    at the piano

    the fat women
    trotting in a circle

    the boy with crinkled knees
    saying his doctor
    will never change

    asks me for a nickel
    asks me for a pencil

O it's time
traffic is heavy

the bridge-tolls up
I live across two rivers

I've filled
her shopping bag
full of Kools
cookies soft candies
a new robe

      love to the family
      don't forget love to the family

THE COLOR OF NEVILLE BRAND'S FRONT TEETH

It begins in the back of the head,
gathering force like the strangler's
mop in Slam sweeping across the floor.
It changes shape like Willie's
sharpened spoon. You can feel it
between the ribs, it has traveled so
far in so short a time: like emotion
after a month on tranquilizers,
like a calendar nude to the guy
in solitary. At first, it seems
colorless as Louie's narrow hands
that could knit doilies or pick
pockets. It's bruised from the last
kidnapping. It seems to be weeping
in your viscera, under the lights,
denying everything. But give it
a break like the Puerto Rican kid
whose only fault was English,
it'll speak in tongues; it'll
rush to your palate like salt.
It's the kind of rage the toothless
bandits felt when they shot off
Gary Cooper's big left toe and he
still wouldn't talk. By the time
it's in your molars, it's too late:
no good glossing it with Pearl Drops
or prayer. It's so much there,
you taste it biting into plums,
beefsteak tomatoes, your cell-mate's
arm.

WIVES OF GENIUSES

They wear eccentric hats and they listen.
They take children to the wrong museums
and talk too loud. They faint at parties.
They spill coffee on beautiful women.
They wear no panties. They forget books
with unhappy endings, and dream of obituaries.
They sit nude on Formica tables.
They ask your name and put it in diaries.
They write anonymous notes to critics.
They lose old friends like parking tickets.
They answer the phone. They keep their looks
at all hours, and stand in windows, like mirrors.
They sing behind doors. They cook in silence.
They smile like saints in empty churches.

THE VISITORS

They've been
in the guest room
so long
we think
they've died
in their sleep.
But they come out
smiling, his face
frozen & her
hair like straw.
They say the sheets
were torn. We
are ashamed
but they
forgive us.
They admire
our matching
robes, our days
off, our beautiful
skin. We begin
to praise their
eyes, but our coffee
gives them hives,
they scratch,
allergic, they feel
headaches coming on.
The phone rings:
snow ten feet high,
the return flight
is cancelled. Oh
too bad do you mind
please stay. We
apologize:
out of soap, milk,

aspirin, *TV Guide*.
All day they whisper
behind the bedroom
door. That evening
we're caught blushing
in each other's
arms. They didn't know,
o my God. They say
we look so pale.
The sherry is gone,
the lines are down.
We start losing at
poker. We tell
stories of summer
as he fills
the inside straight
& she bluffs
with two pair, we
lose a week's pay.
We moan
about the snow,
the lack of fuel.
Their eyes turn white,
they slump in their chairs,
we carry them to bed.
They complain
of last night's
nightmares, how
police beat them
with sticks &
children laughed.
We kiss them,
they wince.
All night we hear
them breathing like
derelicts on a beach.
We dream our funeral,
a two-car motorcade,

the mourners, he
& she, in top hat,
wrinkled dress,
they're waving,
our dear friends.

PUMAS

The female puma, savage queen in heat,
is backing him against the wall of brick,
her tail alive and straight up high, while he's
in a crouch, in a cage, low as her feet,
trying to nip her heels like a bruised snake.
She moans and turns over, but it looks all
wrong, her fluffy thighs opening like wings,
and he springs up to his ledge of oak boards.
His wooden stare is fixed on writhing birds,
his brain is circling like a bird afraid,
the king of fathers flying slow in heat.
He alights among the stiff bars of darkness,
swat! swat! She's an upright queen!
His bought mate, mirror, is now his fear,
her quick left jab prickling alive, her sideway
snarl. And fragile dreams die in his jaws.
It's eyeball to eyeball, and spit to spit,
the wicked lash of tails that break a glass.
The king is scratching scarlet ribbons on
his queen. Her fangs are naked with disgust.

WIDOW

It happens in ways I never expect,
like hailstones in summer. Going
uphill on the bike, I snap the chain.
In the tub, shaving my legs, I cut
my throat on my ankle. I sweat nightly,
pull back the blankets, see my
husband just lying down in the mirror.
I burn my hand on the iron
I test with spit: the children tumble
in from the yard with a dead bird.
I pretend, alone.   I cook
for pale guests seen only at 10 p.m.
They forget to wipe their mouths,
chattering like starlings. I bang
the table and they disappear, black
coffee spilled on the white tablecloth.
I've given up smoking, I try push-ups;
for lungs and double chin, I stand
on my head: watching the late news,
the bombs falling up the sky, the men
ascending in their bloody uniforms.

GIMPEL THE FOOL

*"What about the judgment in the
world to come?" I said.
"There is no world to come."*

ISAAC BASHEVIS SINGER

You got born somehow, your hands
already bigger than the midwife's,
laughter winging its way to Cracow.
They told you the crow in the cemetery
was your father. But you were a goat
tied back of the rabbi's barn, eating
a tinhorn's excuses, everyone's garbage.
Children said, quick, the graves are opening,
Gimpel, bring shoes, the dead have sore feet.

You married the town whore, who kept
more lovers under her bed than there
were uncles in Frampol. At dawn,
when your eyelids were glued shut
and sticky as bread dough, she said:
"Does the moon rise in the morning?"
So you boiled cabbage, scrubbed floors,
your lap grew wet with bastard kids.
You slept on your stomach and heard wolves.

Then your wife died and came back
in a dream: black seeds between her teeth.
She told you there was no bread like
your bread. Scared you out of home,
cash, and Sabbath hat. *Schnorrer*,
happy beggar, you deceived no one
but the Angel of Death asking which way
to the ghetto of Warsaw. You told him
turn left into the field where sages eat filth.

II

FREUD'S LAST DREAM

He's lying back on the couch
analyzing the fact of lying
on the couch: telling Ernest,
also bald, sitting behind him,
that Papa smelled like new shoes.
What did he think of that?
Ernest weeps. No weeping!
Things aren't so black. Have a
cigar. He saved a few things
from Berggasse 19: cigars, hankies,
Martha's beautiful eyes. Was that
the second time he said beautiful?

His bowel movements have been poor.
Last night someone told him
that for elimination raw spinach
is better than cooked goose.
He laughs. He groans. Ernest
is writing something down,
but he objects: it's his
impacted wisdom teeth the lady
dentist said wouldn't grow
back. Women shouldn't be allowed
to say wouldn't or shouldn't.
They had no gift for the subjunctive.

Ernest says he's confusing
the English future. He shrugs.
They had to purge society
of bed-wetters, find men with
beautiful jaws who could explain
themselves. Women only sat around,
unaware of what they're missing.

But he feels faint: he wishes
this were a dream of sunlight,
in a boat of bullrush reeds,
and he were floating down the Tiber,
into Rome, into a woman's hands.

THE ARTIFICE

It is a garden within walls
chromium roses glint in the headlights'
indirect moonlight
quotes from Emerson flicker in neon signs
a porcelain bluejay screams on the hour
I spray lacquer on the wooden beetles
I dip like a chemical bird
who cannot fall through glass
the birdsong tapes warble from the dead
tree twisted round with Woolworth ivy
a flag flutters in the wind of a restaurant fan
the bluejay screams and muzak pours from the statue
of a Siamese cat   why am I kneeling to his mouth?
You pose in a mural unattached to the wall
no shadow falls behind you
I am running on the sinking turf never
quite reaching you who fade into the wall
in bas-relief your hands' ridges almost lifelike

LOSING

I complained about having no shoes
my feet disappeared

I ignored my children on weekends
they ran into Monday

I told my wife I was too tired
she nailed up my closet

I sneezed when the roses came early
they grew under my bed

I kicked the door of my office
it fell into the river

I gave all my money to the poor
I found lice in my hair

On the corner of forty-second street
I dreamed I was happy

LATE MORNING

So I do not get up. I avoid myself,
sheathed in blankets like an Indian
woman. I roll over, an old drunk,
I hear myself breathing the deep,
stertorous dreams in which I succeed,
saying, "Nothing matters." I am my
father, home from work again, and my
wife is puzzled. She tries the remedies
of love, gives me vitamins and good report.
She thinks I need more rest because I
tell her so. I am ill in slothfulness,
in fatigue that deepens with sleep.
I am the grizzled switchman with wino
breath, watching the men lay new tracks
and get up steam: a blue locomotive
charging into my shack-station dream.
I wave them past, holding sacks of mail,
the letters never received, the denials
I've written to the men who cannot read.
I see the graffiti on the station wall.
"You will never forgive yourself."

THE KNUCKLER

We knew your stooped figure in Astoria Park,
knuckle-baller, your hand slow & disdainful
on the diamond beneath the TriBoro Bridge,
fingers forking behind your back. Whatever you
threw wobbled in the air like a soap bubble.
Your mother was the nicest woman in a yard
full of cukes & tomatoes. She bought you aquariums,
little oxygen pumps, a Schwinn, blowups of father.
She thought you too thin. She bought you huge
mittens, big-shoulder coats, while the McDonald
brothers spit on the metal doors of grocery cellars
where you slipped. Anyone at all could find
you in Mendel's, at the magazine rack, slipping
girlies between the pages of *Sports Illustrated*.

All those years, you waited for a fast sign:
a wave from the blonde divorcee in her bedroom
across the driveway. Through Woolworth binoculars,
webbing of blinds, you learned the moles & fine
track of her spine, the rayon slide of her buttocks:
her hands behind her back unhooking a fullness
in your head, behind your eyes, in your throwing hand
that had only a knuckler, only an odd way of holding on.
We couldn't hit you at all in those days,
the gray & muggy afternoons when the ball should
have carried into the East River. We popped up,
we grounded out, the boys from Seymour's Hardware,
& Baker's Garage, & Queeco's Beer, we whiffed in
sunlight, or under cumulus, in the shadow of a long bridge.

But she died suddenly, thirty-eight, a bad heart:
released from your grip, writhing in a midnight glare.
It was obviously your fault. You stopped going
to Mendel's. Sold your Schwinn. Gave up fishing

for minnows in the bay near La Guardia: that airport
built on garbage, carriage wheels, father's shoes.
You stopped catching killies in bent window-screens,
stopped bringing them home alive in tomato cans,
& pouring them into the tank with your tropical fish,
like common children among angels, while your guppies
with the bulbous eyes gave birth & ate their young
beneath the 25¢ pink plaster bridges. You took apart
the pumps. You began to focus on empty windows, sparrows.
All morning, all afternoon, we hit you, O we hit you.

SIBLINGS

When the body
is an empty suit in the closet
I whisper I am
and know that I will not be

and when I am not
anywhere to be seen or heard
will my last thought
become the first cry
of a baby girl in Peru
born and held in the web of my death

as I too was born
of an English coal miner
gasping his life into the chain
through me
in the links of flowers
grown from rotted mouths

My sister
you will leave the locked room
your deaf madness
our father's terrified soul
the dark bird
will fly out of your mind
to become a condor in the Andes

a lizard breaking birds' eggs
yolks dripping from his jaws

MIDDLE AGE

Dive into it, into a belly:
a fat uncle's joke at a wedding.
Into the navel & obscene
folds of gravity: visceral
in a blurred love of detail. The dreamt-of
old man on a bench, grinning:
& she twitches past. Catch me, you old bugger!

My cousin, the artisan's
objets d'art in pewter:
good-news dog, metal-slit jaws
holding a want ad;
& "together": a boy & girl
under a gray tree.
An oyster closing.

After the burial,
a new feeling. Your arms
never so good as now, & my interest
in drawn shades: as if
a young girl behind the shade,
undressing, dreaming of *him*, & I would
step in there, behold!

CAVE PAINTINGS

A one-legged bird in profile, short of beak,
off balance. The lance in my abdomen
like a needle in the egg that is my body,
& one eye: I see the long antelopes that fly
on the opposite wall, a thumbprint of light,
your ocher eye. You are the humpbacked male,
rearing, your genitals hung too high & behind,
the soul of cat, the joints of wings in your jaws.
O if I could move, disengage the lance,
I would travel across, flutter behind you,
my eye would fill with blood & be afraid.
You would turn outward in darkness
& around, to face me, hornless & smooth,
we would place ourselves eye over eye.

But I am the blow to your hearing,
the bowl that will be made of your skull,
the eye-sockets of your enemy
rising in the midnight fire. I am the dream
of your skin hung from the leafless tree.

SURGERY

The dwarf nurse takes my temperature.
There's a pencil in my mouth. Already,
I'm eating my words, when she turns
to my five-year-old daughter dressed
in white curtains like a bride. It
doesn't matter, she's the doctor: here's
my new jellybean heart stuffed in a
thimble. I'm the cat mewing in doll's
clothes, ready to die, and she blows
into the thimble to bring my heart alive,
tells me I can't move, only babies cry.
I'm in surgery on the bathroom floor.
The green light darkens on the wall.
Am I in Bellevue? The medication trays
rattle in the hallway. Tug whistles
are moaning on the river like old women.
The dwarf nurse winks. She adjusts her
brassiere. My daughter is counting her
fingers. A gong sounds. "Calling Dr. No."
What have I denied? I'm marked with
lipstick, sticky X, and spit. Physician
with my wife's brow, my brother's grin,
she's digging in, unclasping my sternum.
I'm an open ship's hold taking cargo of
turtle hearts and she's lowering
her thimble on a thread into the hole
closing slowly as a cat's iris.
Someone is flushing a toilet.
The nurse sprinkles sugar on my stomach.
A cat rushes up and licks it off.
Everyone nods. The PA system plays the wedding march.
My daughter puts a monocle over the open wound,
slips skin around the edges of a glass hole.

I'm finished. I lift my head and see into it.
I can look into the picture-window egg of my soul
where snow falls forever on the tiny house.

III

RELEASE

1

Sunday, in my office,
opposite the beige brick church,
I look up from the blank page.
The four clocks in the four faces
of the tower are telling different
times. Each way I turn,
the hands of the separate clocks
of the separate selves
pose into this and that
posture, dancers
test and change their gestures,
turning four faces one by one
to me, each face that I fear
to become or to come out of.

2

There I am
in the photo
wearing a sawtooth beanie,
throwing a pink rubber ball at the camera:
1945, the fleet's coming up the Hudson,
barooming salutes. The Pom . . . Pom . . . Pom
is not the noise I expected,
not ripping the air.
I throw the ball at the camera
which is being held by Mr. Weber
home from Italy with a wooden leg.

Profile: boy with hooked nose,
hair curved over forehead and behind ear;
silver jacket with fur collar.
Some mistake of the film.

Strange exposure.
The boy stares
at something beyond the frame.

Is that me, fat and blond,
held up in my father's arms?
I clutch the lapel of his pin-stripe suit
while the roof's
black tar and open chimneys
devour the sunlight.

Alice poses on the roof,
my sister: just
plump enough
to swell out beneath
the edges of her bathing suit.
TV antennas poke at the sky like broken claws.
Her English jaw hangs heavy on her smile.

We're sitting in the bright sun
of Uncle Charlie's backyard
near the el's spiderweb shadows.
In short pants,
propping Danny on my lap,
I scowl at the camera
and wonder why brothers cry all night.
His pug nose defies
definition.

Nowhere do I find my mother
married.   Another roof picture:
almost seven years before
her daughter will be born.
She's 20: her white dress
stark against the black roofs and open doorways.
The turn in her eye is coy,
evading the camera's eye.
The frills on her short sleeves are pretty.
The Depression is still on.

There I am
on the beach
holding my brother Stevie.
He squints at the sun and reflects
the scowl of my father,
who is propped on his elbows in the sand.

Sometimes they all seem dead
though they try to pursue me into marriage
and my thirty-fifth year and though I often
wake with my father in my arms   trying to save him
from his early death   and I still cannot find
a picture of my mother married and the coy eye
evades me in my dreams and my sister grins on the roof.

3

Instructor of English, appointed 1967
(smiling)

No, this can't be right

Mr. Allman shines white on black
on the door of 205 Eddy Hall

a trapped hawk claws
the back of my eyes

I walk on naked feet
from one abstraction into
another   coughing up feathery bones

   diplomas curl on the wall

Married,
one child, daughter, age six

4

For Eva whom I describe
as the nymph leaping out of the summer night
into my room:

why should I mark you with words
like savage tattoos?

The Jerome Avenue el squeals
in the valley beneath us
sparking the midnight
our veins thunder   they thunder
love's release

all night
the hollow-eyed white bird
calls

my love
my love
damn these words
what are words
what are words
rags stuffed into a mouth

it seems so long ago
we married

5

The future holds her in a box,
a small woman with hair turning white.
Even in death, her eye turns away.

The mad don't get madder
biting the spoons in their mouths
(tranquilizers steam in the blood
like fog on a tropical river, the air
fills with the cries of beautiful birds).

The clocks on the four faces of a tower
turn their sibling hours into lust,
meditation, fear, and a blank face:
the nothing that fills in each minute
like a sound that congeals in the air,

a noise that is seen, suddenly, twisting
into a vapor, a thread, that passes away.

6

I awaken to the midnight bird
who ruffles his wings, preening
(no humans in my dream,
only the sun here, the bird).
On the tips of my fingers
there are tiny photographs
and my eyes open their lenses
to let something fly out
fluttering toward carnival mirror
camera closeups: gyrating faces,
big noses, small eyes, rectangular mouths.
Sudden silence.   The sun's myriad
bells toll out light
that beams upward from my cool sheets,
my wife's hips.   I arise spreading my arms
like a frail bird running into a thin breeze,
I'm aloft, above the glinting Hudson River,
riding upwards on a voice I still cannot hear,
impelled on its beautiful pure lung force,
up, up, up, my brain softly exploding,
fingers stroking my head, my eyes,
my beak.   There is wreckage everywhere
washed up on the mud islands, where the sun's knives
cut through water: beer cans, twisted logs, scummy
weeds, curled strips of exposed film. I see the
body of a dog and I scream for joy.

7

The face appears on the blank page:
my mother's eyes;
the nose hooked like her mother's.
The jaw belongs to some Victorian

Englishman, or a coal miner
who looks like D. H. Lawrence.
It's me.

The Methodist Church
turns a paler beige year by year.
The rectangular tower
keeping four points of time
turns in a circle
and hands on the clocks
give their gestures
in the repetition of hours.

I hear the fleet coming downriver
in fog, barooming salutes,
while the tall boats, draped in black,
carry the dead to sea.

IV

THE SOUL PLAYS YOU BET YOUR LIFE

But I'm the famous one, wiggling
my eyebrows, tapping my cigar,
asking her what question would
she stake all on, what category
good at: Flowers of Tibet?
Diseases of New Jersey?
She's coy, edging away, unmarried.
Never had what you call a job.
Dates older men with bad hearts
and insurance. I can't believe it,
lovely thing like her (want something
on the side, eh? rolling my eyes).
She likes movies with a message,
strawberry malts that foam over.
Her half sister was the quadroon
with bleached hair, in black undies,
who took up in New Orleans with
unnamed politicians. She herself
at twelve was had by an uncle,
at thirteen by an aunt. Later,
in two-piece Jantzen, sequin shoes,
she was Miss Used Car of Tupelo.
She knows the songs from old musicals,
does a little dance, does her imitation
waltz and call of the Depressed Canary.
I'm flipping the white cards of her
categories, her fears, her memories
of cities with rivers, high winds,
bridges that fell, the worst tornados.
She looks pale as a first-nighter
dreaming of broken legs and the hook.
I come at her suddenly bristling:
a booking agent with impatient
mustache. My top question is worth

a two-week cruise on the *Eastern Star*
that never enters the 12-mile limit.
All the Black Jack and Craps
she can handle, all the gigolos
from here to Rio, Big Bands,
top singers, unlimited cash.
The smoke from my cigar settles
around us like a fog, as I tell her
I'm the consolation prize.

THE SOUL GROWN LAZY

Dressed in black &
overweight, her voice damp:
she sighs, telling me of father
off on a big job overseas,
papa & his brothers.
I'm showing her the night city,
frowsy shops in alleys.
Little boys pick my pockets
& signs hang in windows
of restaurants: Credit Good.
No aunts behind us,
no Registrar, no mayor dozing
beneath a floppy hat, just
her loneliness, huge & flabby,
leaning against me.
I feel sweet. I kiss
the fourth fold of her neck,
my hand travels the ring
of her waist, I find
the many paths to her breasts.
She's worrying: what if we're
caught what if the police
come screaming red-faced
into this alley what if
she's really no good eating
pizza & doughnuts drinking
vanilla malteds watching
TV all day sleeping waking
up eating the blankets filling
the tub with ice cream her
lips always caked with
chocolate frosting will I
love her will I love her?

THE SOUL WALKS OUT

His fever up to 103, while she quoted others:
her walking out now just wasn't right.
Such thin histrionics, the way she dropped
her box of beauty marks, leaving stars everywhere;
counting out unused Pokerino coupons, kissing
the prize velvet dog. Hadn't it been a good time?
But she didn't care: suitcase crammed with hard
times, hard candies, fake eyelashes, her Gideon.
So he'd seen the secret moles on her back, plucked
one true souvenir hair and taped it on his wall.
Was that so much? Listen, he was no saint.
He was going to sleep, sick, air-conditioning high.
She just better not be here when he woke up.

KINSHIP

In the first dream, it is winter:
you walk on snowshoes through the woods.
A deer's carcass hangs from an oak
& your hand enters its visceral cavity:
cold. You hunt for the knife in snow.
You know you will be hunted into evening.

You run barefoot into the second dream,
wide-eyed, now you're swimming upriver,
impeded by the clothes you sleep in.
Your father is waving on the bank,
dry, the trees falling behind him,
he can't hear your warning, your halloo,

& you are nervous in the third dream,
on a kitchen chair, helping mother
peel apples for a pie you won't like.
She says, wash your face. Now. Quick.
Your father returns from the river.
You cut yourself. She says, see. See.

You have nowhere to go. Five years old,
hiding in doorways, grinding your teeth.
Your brother jogs past you on the street
but you say you are the only child
& he runs into a lamppost. You
howl like a wolf. Mother combs your hair.

Father is sad. Your sister has just died.
The funeral feast is crowded with police
& mice run up your legs. Father complains:
what's for dessert? Mother lifts the bowl,
the large brown bowl filled with beets,
her hands splotched as with a rash.

In the next dream, you are gaining weight,
asleep in a chair. Your loved one
covers you with a white sweater
& brings you a dish of fruit.
Scent of lilacs: outside, the willow weeps,
you are weeping, you want everything to last.

No family in the next dream: you sweat,
grown thin, you are on a train
during the dog days, your friends are married.
The blurred stations receive no call,
your picture in the ad above you,
toothpaste in your hand. You are a failure.

Lost, following the moss on trees
into sleep: no way out of this dream.
Beautiful bodies surround you,
luminous, in pain, they close in for comfort.
You answer their eyes with your eyes.
Nothing matters. Lust seizes you.

It is too late in the last dream,
struggling in the river. No one is near.
Father on the shore, paring his nails;
mother airing blankets under the trees.
You swallow water, & your lungs
bloom beside you on the lily pads:

you will imagine blue herons;
you will hear the rustle of blood;
pale children will call your name,
as trout break the surface, as geese cry,
as light settles everywhere upon the water,
you are swimming toward home.

THE MILD

You had almost
forgotten these
animals: their
see-through eyelids.

They look at you
and ammonia
fills the room.
You owe them nothing.

The long blue
snouts at the
window, inquiring
tongues. Where

is your notebook,
write this
down. *They stare.*
You feel

yourself
bent over the
table, your
hair white:

the animals
slowly turn
away and begin
adorning

themselves
with sprigs
of weigelia.
They sit like bears,

fish wriggling
in their paws.
You didn't know
they had hungers.

You write,
of course. Now
the animals
are mounting

your abandoned
car, whimpering
and pumping
their eager

hips. You write,
stop, but all
they do is lick
each other's

eyes.
Your notebook
becomes
a blur,

you smell
dark plums,
the rank odor
of wet fur.

You begin naming
the shapes
of their tracks:
foliate, lovely.

You see
their flanks
gleaming
in the river.

You feel
the ache of
what it means
to know them.

You close your
eyes and stare
through your lids
at flat fields

of snow. The animals
gone into the woods
and gone their prints
as they make them.

A FORMER LIFE

A narrow cobbled street:
my house with the slate roof
and upstairs rooms with fireplaces.
I'm looking down on the gaslights
paling in the street: dawn, cool air,
the footsteps of the Watch.
I hear my youngest daughter
coughing up the last of illness.
My son is up, preparing the stove,
the hot water for his tea.
Soon he will go to the shop,
his work as apprentice: the fine
tools; the ridged detail of silver;
snuff boxes; plates that will be
heirlooms; memorial cups.
I lean into my wife's body,
I face the ceiling. In this life,
I sleep on the left side of the bed,
my left hand is missing a middle finger,
my two daughters have dark eyes,
my wife is a large woman
who loves music and my tenor voice.

A DEATH

He makes the merest sound
rising from the dust
an old man sitting up
his eyes closing like apertures
on the sunlit meadow

picnickers spread a tablecloth
he lurches forward
steps on the little girl's hand
he can't lift his foot out of the salad
they smile and ask him to sit
the father gives him a cigar
mother buttons his shirt
they stick a chicken leg in his mouth
he grins and

they jump up and down
they knock him over in the grass
he chokes on a bone
they turn him over and over
he's out of breath
being rolled downhill to the river
clover stuck to his greasy lips

he lies with one hand in the water
the girl whirls in her tutu
coming over she laves his face
blows him a kiss
tadpoles leap from his fingertips
he stands
his feet turn into cucumbers

the parents clap their hands three times and
the girl curtsies at her image in the river and

the old man crawls into a tree
and the family disappears

what is the wood singing
eyes in the branches
the roots moving

FILLING THE STRAIGHT

I look up from the table
but the mirror above his head
is black as the window
of a whorehouse. I can't see
his hearts or clubs, my own cards
transparent. He reads all my
backward movements. I skim
three chips from the stack
that levels like grain in silos.
I smell a fermentation. Hooch.
It's the Sour Doughs pushing closer
behind me, gray bits falling
in my lap, the clay of poor claims
from their fingernails. I'm losing
the ranch, my buckboard, the Mexican
saddle, while dance-hall girls
snap their garters. The Derringer
strapped to my calf
slides down into the bone of my left
ankle: it's the pain of riding
the north 40, swinging my foot
sideways into a fence post,
into a blunt tooth. But I smile.
I call. I lose. He deals.
He snaps his fingers: the waiter
brings a shot of red-eye,
wearing the elastic that keeps
sleeves high, hands blue.
O my joints are stiff. I've
been here for hours, days, weeks,
since May, since the drought
and sick cattle. I'm drawing
a Queen to my one-eyed Jack,
remembering my wife's polka-dot
dress, the army of sheepmen
guarding the river.

DEPARTURE

It is travel. It is not
a dream of falling into the same
river. It is Chagall's winged
woman offering a bouquet by the Eiffel Tower.

We depart, knowing the bus driver's
arms will not fall off.

Children will not harm each other,
their daisy eyes lifted to the moon.

The dead animals will rise
& trot along the white line
as we reach into paper bags for peaches.

Our fingers twitch with the memories
of knitting. We doze to accustomed sounds.

Water. Trees. Steam. The unicorn snorting.

INTO

dream walker
guides you to the Sand Hills
where the white buffalo
shy from your bad odor

the lost wife
does not recognize you
here the dry strings of meat
pour rivulets from your hand

the stone you throw into the river
is my eye looking up looking down
if it floats & wolf trots away
you will be dead only four days

58

AWAY & TOWARDS

spirit of bear emerging in tall grass
walking four ways in the wind each side
of you & before & behind yet falling away
like That Above Person in the camp of ghosts

deadly to you the arrow of the Snake
passes through him like a bone needle
O you think this feeling is bad
the dream of water rising to your chin

the turtle rising milk-eyed in the river
where you turn narrow & selfish your soul
a long thin shadow wavering in the current
body dreaming of the travel north in dream

RETURN

I hear wolf behind me
the footsteps of hunger
I am coming back
through deer shit & badger smell

to the edge of dark water
lit by bear's ghost singing
the edge of dark water
where turtle descended four times

rising with new mud
humped on his back
before the birds had names
& muskrat could swim

I carry grandmother's bones
lower a leg bone into the lake
I am here O king of fish
to be swallowed mid-sentence

to knock thin ribs in the oily darkness
my feet slipping on your soft organs
the water bubbling near your gills
I bang your heart with her bone

until you die coughing me up
the other side of this lake
I will be the undigested part
lifted by heron high above trees

dropped into the clearing
beyond water & tar pools & man bones
I will gleam in the withered grass
like a sarvis berry found by bear

V

NANA'S VISIT

She hid her bottle of port
in the kitchen washtub
and we'd catch her lifting
the porcelain lid, reaching in:
we heard a swishing, and remembered
the smell of wet newspapers
in her icebox; the hall toilet
that gargled as you froze
on the seat and strange footsteps
went past. And suddenly father
was shouting. O his mother was drunk again,
singing her old vaudeville songs,
unloosening her stiff legs.
You could almost see the music hall
lit up, the Indian clubs whirling
like a halo around her head,
up went the left leg, up the right.
We saw her steamer trunk,
the pleated panties like pink
carnations, the sharp edges
of yellow contracts, a photo
of her father, his white moustache
hung like the cliffs of Dover.
We heard the men of Tipperary
whistling would she do it again,
and she did, against the painted scenery,
the flat trees of Eden shimmering
in gaslight. Up went her skirt,
out went her bum. We heard applause,
watched her kick off her shoes
in grand finale. She snuffed out
a row of candles with her naked feet.

WIDOWER

The scent comes out of the blue
level he sees himself upon
like a deer poised upwind
the change coming down the heights of snow
he is stretched on a blue
bedspread a three-way lamp turned
up blazing white the TV eye winked shut
his daughter dreaming of white muffs
he drifts in flu's fever not himself
away he slips away into her white arms
sweat clinging to a two-day beard
the stubbled slopes of his mind
alive with deer leaping the blue
abyss he falls peacefully to death in

Arising at eight clear of the chattering
teeth and thin blankets fever breaks through
he tells the world it is too soon
too late the time bends
his back with irregular stones
he has a daughter to survive Emergency
Rooms his white face breaking in the glass
not the comical groans actors make
he has controlled all that
pulling the X of disease into shapes
he rolls in his hands like the lather
clouds warming his face beneath
he has so much to die for differences of
philosophy he dare not whisper to mirrors

Night animals have gone behind his
eyes he's a man descending mountains
feet tingling from an old frostbite
or is it a thaw some native bare entry

onto palm leaves like the long-legged
women padding down office corridors
or is the festive dream on the wall
a bloom of pasted flowers over cracks
mere design 39¢ a foot fading
his daughter is ready now for school
he buttons her coat and gloved hands
touch the facial flaw he cannot disown
he tells her to enter new geographies
she must sit and learn of the Spanish poor

THE FIXER

I snip the appliance cord
mother whips you with
put a rubber thimble
on stepfather's fore-
finger that prods you awake
to take out the dog
I shrivel brother's arms
so he will not punch you
beneath Gallagher's window

I close the fissure
in your upper lip take
away the tongues of boys
who imitate you I also
take away your lungs
because you hum absent-
mindedly at uncle's funeral
I take away your six-
finger knife bring you
home from prison without
a skeletal face give

your girl fat Patricia
a dead father's thin
waist I unhook her brassiere
here is the love you
needed to give and to
get here is the toll
money for exit 3 before
you crash in fog in
the lane for trucks only

THE LOST WIFE

He's resting in the secondhand chair:
splinters. Like the barn door in Kansas.
Hattie's antiques: broken lamps, the gramophone,
daguerrotypes of great-great aunts.
The blonde wheat women are calling to him
in the harvest of owls, reaping balls of hair.

He dreams his son climbing a tree,
ripping his pants. He dreams his brother
lifting a rock over his head: go ahead,
he says, bash me to Chicago.

Mother is the white figure in the vegetable garden,
his father smoking in the truck without wheels:
whiskey bottles tumbled among the squash,
children running in and out of the pole beans,
the bucket unravelling with a hiss into the well.

She's in the mirror behind him: the dark woman
he loves, the woman of the plains,
with plaited hair, arising in the smell
of hides hung over night fires.

He's running through the dust
into a valley of snakes: he knows
such spines; the wriggling knots;
the pits of Manitoba, himself
pictured in the *Geographic*
when he knew how to catch
and hold things behind the eyes.

She's there, he knows it: between speech,
tooth and nostril, like a snake
he draws in the exact register

of her heat. His nerves quiver with evasion.
His mouth grows wet with the taste of her skin
on the small of her back. He passes her once,
then twice. She is around every outcropping
of rock; always there, hands at her sides,
eyes dilating with pain in the X-ray negative of the sun.

RECONCILIATION

In darkness, like a camera, your shutter wide:
as if fathers coming upstairs could be seen,
their hands never closing the solid oak doors.
And their letters said the right thing:
"Daughter, I'm coming home. Dream of rivers."
You do. You want the exact moment
of arrival. The long water behind you
flat with dust: the sky embedded in it,
two people in a boat, their white hands
like bait in the water. You want to see him
freshly out of there: hair shaggy with weeds,
eyes like quartz, the black tunnel in his groin
filled with snails. And if he tried to speak,
you would interpret his pain to him.
You would clean him up and fit him
with a living heart. You would be
his child with the crystalline eyes.
You would step at last out of your negative.

YOU OWE THEM EVERYTHING

Their fingers numb in thimbles,
eyes dim with hems, their front teeth gone,
they mean well. You give them old lamps.
You give them the room over the garage.
They wash your kitchen windows, looking in.
They smile like maiden aunts with lace
collars and hearing aids. They nod like doctors.
You thank them for the years on their
knees in office vestibules, the wrung-out hands,
the checks for your law books, the debts
they paid with Irish brogues in old movies.
Even your Porsche coughs in their presence.
Some of your children ask who they are
and you speak of Slavic ladies in cabbage
fields, the Haitian grandmothers dumping ashtrays.
You name the widows with varicose veins
and prominent sons who visit twice a year;
chug-a-lug maids in Hotel Edison, connoisseurs
of abandoned wine; sisters of vaudeville stars.
You hear their jangled nerves ring up in dry-
goods stores. You hear them praise children
moved to Wisconsin. They are the lost nannies
in Victorian novels, the housekeepers with rings
of keys, who put the cool cloth to hysteric
brows, who soothe like cellos in the great hall.
They know they accept everything. They know
you wake in your middle-age sweating, thinking
of them. They smoke Lucky Strikes. They buy Wonder Bread.

FOR ONE WHO MOVED AWAY

It's a converted barn you rent here,
the town small, outside Duluth; high
windows, double doors racked by wind
off Lake Superior. The icebound schools
are open every day: but you don't rise
a dumb oak above the fast talkers of P.S. 70.
Your wife's bleary with late movies,
big on Jack Daniel's, her touch of class.
The first husband's son has kicked in
both headlights of the old Ford
behind the shed: you carry dark circles
under your eyes; you laugh at your daughters,
those tame bears upright on bicycles
in snow. Things roll off their backs,
names skid into drifts, Big Dope, Meathead.

It gets quiet along the ice line
of Canada, before the world cracks
in half, spring breaks through:
but on the docks your mammoth hands
catch the spill of the St. Lawrence
Seaway. You bring home grain dust
on your pants, smudges of ore on shoes,
the world's resources almost yours.
You're nothing without the Union,
the beers, the friend who's half-Chippewa.
But you don't sweat things like Algebra
and wrong answers we gave you; driving
west like a Dude smoking cigarillos,
teaching the son how to crumple beer-
cans in one hand, steering with the other.

GERIATRICS

A warm
December she
feels a bit
dry he's
at the wheel
waiting the
drawbridge
rising she
listens
to groaning
hinges old
birds' nests
falling
the Pontiacs
thrumming in
place the brick
factory's
fuming
pipes tall
as silos
rising
from red
dust the Mobil
barge
thumping
through oil
slick it's
such a long wait

THE WARD WIFE

I line them up, your colleagues
with inky fingers, nephews
adjusting their ties and ten
pounds heavier, the office girl
reeking of the tuna-fish sandwiches
you shared with her. I organize
your visitors as if their loving
needed some rehearsal, the right
inflection: before you lose
your lines, smiling, clicking
your tongue at the gray man
in the bed next to yours
who is also dying. I turn down
the sound of the TV always on
above you. Our dumb show
without commercials is not
as real; the how-are-you's
useless as the wrapped stems
of get-well roses trickling
in a vase. Nor is there any
winning here, any prize blooming
on a lighted board. The soft
chimes over the PA announce
someone's advance; the doctors
called are less handsome
than their TV doubles
always in conference with blondes,
always unfaithful, getting
divorced, saving their nephews
with remarkable operations.
And I'm your English maid,
your third wife putting a bent straw
in a glass.   Everyone leaves,
happy that you are happy
with your morphine smile.

But you rummage me like a file,
search my nylon openings
for cool memories. You ask me
have you died yet. Would I
give you a shave. You admire
my paisley blouse like a garden
through which no one can move.
And I lather you with hissing lime,
scrape you cheek to jowl,
the long thighs of my movement
near and far as the hips
of angels, my wet hands
like fallen leaves catching
rain.   You're almost done.
I'm dusting you smooth,
patting on talc. You're
fresh as the baby we never had,
and I ache all over
in the deep labor of loving you.
You can hardly see me.
You're muttering. I'm the homely
Audubon girl on your father's
ranch, my pigtails forward,
over my cleavage. I'm sitting
the fence, a dry bird's nest
in my lap. You're in chaps
and plaid, your lungs almost clear.
You lift your legs to mount me,
you have me moving now
on blunt plateaus; your days
in Montana; the year of the new
sorrel and mother's bad heart.
I'm the spotted mare carrying you
to the loneliness of rivers,
the high cattails, the oozy reeds,
the sky beginning to flicker
above us, as we find our way
to the frail eggs of geese.

HIS CREMATION

Last night they came out of the fog
back of hospitals, from a dream,
Sioux warriors in dark business suits
smelling of creosote. They said
nothing, walking up the wooded
hill. How much dead weight could I be?
They tied me to the high platform
in the trees, where owls would
rest on my eyes but never wake me.
The wind carried away their song.

Today I'm almost back where I
left off, old Prof in baggy pants,
just a kind of ordinary
tin can between the potted plants,
imprint on a pad from the page
before. I think my wife must be
home, sewing, in an open gown
like mine. I'm an excited child
lurching over bedrails, slipping
past the nurse, looking for a door.

I smell an acrid something not
me. Smokestacks? Parking lots? I give
them up and look from windows at
the road. It curves into distance.
Perhaps Wagner on stereo
when I tilt in a box and go
downhill on stage in front of friends
through the swinging doors, the glowing
mouth busy behind the curtain
spitting out gold teeth and ashes.

FINDING THEM

I'm looking
for them everywhere
I step out
the back door
of the bus
hatless half-
bald I've been
here before
the old women
eating
knockwurst under
the trees looking
into the canal
spitting out
bits of bone
it's illegal
feeding the
fish this
way the men in
white caps
are dragging
the women away
ah there they
are my wife
& daughter
on the rot-
wood pier
throwing
avocados into
the water
a long green
arc
I'm stepping
off Oh

my daughter's
bobbing below
& the see-
through fish
with sides like
sandwich wrap
are leaping
up swallowed
on my wife's
hands her fingers
shine through
their ribs

PERSONAL

Florida woman wide-hipped pretty fair
condition mid-40s never married
seeks slender man 24-35
moderate barfly OK no politics
poor skin or Oedipists
needs loving right man open to moves
marriage likely am growing
tired of long-walk widowers
who don't smoke or swear
I sleep late lie sulk nag am bad
dreamer with mortgage paid for
central A/C who loves antique Tennyson
no Hemingways please
no Cuban spies
no hectic loners with bony fingers
used to women like clams
no fishy symbolists please or
menorah saints giving orders
good talkers old-time venters
needed but I don't listen after
1 a.m. yes I'm top-heavy I've
never tried this before
good eater over 5'9" won't
go hungry hidden yard available
photo a must small feet come to me
lover of wrought iron faithful as Friday
will meet you halfway in the mail
will walk to Miami to greet you

THE WEEPER

I'm doing it openly at a Formica table
in Bickford's the waitress gives me hankies
the Puerto Rican family is waving & nodding
 my father is the counterman scraping
  his shoes poor man he steps in everything
my mother the immigrant woman mopping
the floor I weep into her bucket's milky
water O look it's never too late mother
 but the bouncer in tuxedo's coming at me

cry he says keep crying out you go you
drifter who let you in unshaven your feet
poking through sneakers sit up straight
 I see my daughter outside dancing for pennies
  I'm knocking on the window hey you hey you
my father says close your eyes we're counting
the receipts go to sleep your mother is tired
leaning on the mop O it's my sister O lucky
 brother don't stuff napkins in your mouth

quick a menu waitress where am I listen here
I am below the Saturday blue special baked
fool with hash-browns & week-old lettuce
 bring me death & pancakes bring me something
  before it's too late I can weep for at 25¢
it's my wife blowing her nose it's good she says
O lucky husband no one but you weeps so well
come to bed in the ice days of January in the
 evening beneath the quilt you can cry into my hair

BOY

I battle him on the mountain
he sweeps a giant root through the air
I heave the first stones
where he bleeds he heals instantly

a gust of wind blows my missiles back
my ribs bend in and spring out
we can't hurt enough
the sun wobbling while stars

fall into the lake
then it is spring the eagles
claw our heads we roll down
into the village where grandmother

smokes a pipe watching him
strike me with an elm tree
I hit him with a sycamore
by summer we're deep in corn

he says "enough" he gives me
a horse and soft blanket of wolf-hair
arrows that double in flight a bowl
of clear oil to keep me young forever

I give him a handful of teeth
that burst like pods and white
birds fly off into the sudden rain
into his sudden wound

Library of Congress Cataloging in Publication Data

Allman, John, 1935-
Walking four ways in the wind.

(Princeton series of contemporary poets)
I.   Title.
PS3551.L46W34   811'.5'4   79-83974
ISBN 0-691-06402-4
ISBN 0-691-01359-4 pbk.